Dark Man Blues

Dark Man Blues: the other side

Samuel Rain Benjamin

and

Eric DeVaughnn

INNATE DIVINITY

San Bernardino/Houston

Copyright © 2017 by Samuel Benjamin

All rights reserved under International and Pan-American
Copyright Conventions. Published in the United States by
N/8 Divinity Publishing, San Bernardino, California; Houston, Texas
All of the poems in this collection, are Copyright © by Samuel Benjamin and
are reprinted by permission of Complicated Passions and Dark Man Blues the
Series. No part of this publication may be reproduced, or transmitted in any
form or by any means, electronic, mechanical, photocopying, recording or
otherwise without the written permission of the publisher.
ISBN-13: 978-0-9996018-0-8 (Innate Divinity)
ISBN-10: 0999601806

Edited and formatted by: Eric DeVaughnn

In Loving Memory of Jason Jijja Scott

Brother 2 Brother

12/16/73 - 01/15/17

the pages...

The Dark

1. Black on Blood Stains
2. Back to the future
3. Camouflage
4. Facing Reality
5. Born Free
6. Think About It
7. Never
8. Real Talk in Real Times
9. Holocaust 1619-2017?
10. Once a Slave
11. Will He Lynch Me?
12. Death by Color
13. 13
14. 1492
15. Speak the Truth
16. A New Name
17. The Take Out
18. Private Institutions
19. Painting America

The Man

20. Riding High
21. The Echoes
22. The Game
23. The Symbol
24. The Illusion
25. Man's Last Stand
26. No Reply
27. A Different Me
28. Self, Conversation
29. Telling You Something
30. Color Lines
31. Happenstance
32. Audience Participation
33. Stagnant
34. Dark Man Blues

The Blues

35. Echoes of You
36. Your Mind
37. Loving You
38. The Lines
39. Open Pages
40. Never Can Say No
41. Anticipation
42. My Lovely You
43. The Rest of My Life
44. Did You Know?
45. Finding Complicated Passions
46. Off Paper Love
47. Where I'm Coming From
48. Exposed
49. Captured
50. The Biggest Part of Me
51. Writing to Her
52. Love and the Condition
53. Loving You: part 2
54. A Blind Man's Story
55. Mad Love
56. Only Room 4 2
57. Open Dialogue
58. Safari
59. Word Remedy
60. Beautiful Blindness
61. Like Music
62. Playing Temptation
63. Complicated Passions: After Midnight
64. Lost Inside of You
65. The Written Confessions of DMB
66. Love Wants an Answer
67. The Tale of Dark Man Blues
68. The Bridge
69. The Whisper of My Name
70. Something About Me
71. My Next Book

Extra Content:

Evolve
A Reflection of Who I Am
Dark Girl Magic

The Dark

1. Black on Blood Stains

Can't hide the past

painted pictures of life's conditions

haunting live memories played out

it wasn't me

doesn't have to be

The imprint on asphalt

streets cemetery now our Black Men

our Women suffer swoon

"Is that my child?"

Somebody tell me

what we term this;

shot down

choked out

found dead in a cell

still living this hell

I can see it just so...

that painting looks like my blackness,

labeled... on blood stains

2. Back to The Future

One hundred-and-fifty-year setback
1865 America got checked

reimagine the last century and half
in this time line, we fight back

no more wait and see, no more democracy
no voting for your false sense of reality

damn that! This is gonna be
the big payback

my future intention stands true
these thoughts ring with finality

(it's 3am and you
have pushed the right button!)

3. Camouflage

See it?
the picture disguises itself as TRUTH
America in living color
in black and white

see the liars cover up history TRUTH
is there any surprise
they voted for one of their own?

See the indignation! "I beg to differ!"
you say you're not but
stand with birds of a flocking feather

democrats, republicans
feel free to fact-check me
discover the   TRUTH

we are now faced with a lie
they can no longer   ERASE

see them? see the chameleons?

4. Facing Reality

I could tell you
      many stories

each begins, an
      like old school rhyme
like, once upon a time

do I have your attention?
      because real life
      could be ending.

someone, please pray
we hear names
      hoping it's not family

life is not a given
one day to the next

wrong place
shots fired

(damn...that was close)

5. Born Free

Sixty years of urtication
defining the moments
attempting to define me

manmade landmines
honor war
give grace to grave

I, born this free
was never meant
to be slave

cloak my mind in open cover up
the internet exposes truth
in written lies

the stories old ones told
I know this history ain't mine
why stay? Give me my passport

to freedom

6. Think About It

Dwell on today, then
look back on the way things used to be

400 years of the same story played out live
rewritten history was only to fool his own

"tell a lie enough and they will believe it"
dumb them down and they won't rise

remember when we couldn't read?
are we reading at all, yet?

dwell on today, then consider
how so very like yesterday

7. Never

The truth was all a lie
taught my history that is
thought they could write me out
could erase a past, thought we would

forget

always making up something new
Jim Crow, after school slave special
a textbook on control
its mission statement:

never let them grow
never let them know
who they truly are

8. Real Talk in Real Times

See how reality is playing out

these days, lies broadcast and distract
somebody slipped up

the cat is out of the bag
just across your path
so shoot him

"he had a gun; well, I thought I saw one"

"he didn't follow orders"

"I feared for my life"

reality is
he was black

9. Holocaust 1619-201?

The block in history called slavery
ended but we are still living in it

you say you are free
check the system
from plantation to ghetto living
there is no truth in it
what makes America great?
poverty, barely living?
fighting illegal wars?
No, you have no dignity
you're just that:
formality

he wishes he could change the game
but he's winning Holocaust

10. Once A Slave

Freedom.

At no time in this life have I ever been.
a made-up reality
trapped on a 1619 replay,
no tv, somehow, same channel, same display

1776
the constitution was not written for me
1865 fighting each other to free me?
fact check the reality on that shit

both wore white sheets and
wanted to see you hanging from a tree

seems like yesterday
wants me to forget
it ain't over yet

11. Will He Lynch Me?

This is america's willie lynch legacy
in all her glory
how to make a slave
gave the fear of death
who, living the same story again
in twenty sixteen
his dream, nightmare them, they'll give in.

shoot them dead on TV
let everybody see

the bible said so
control his soul

the willie lynch of old, alive and well
kill black souls and this will be your end:
what goes around
sounds like we've been
willie lynched again

12. Death by Color

Some say

"Not in America! Land of the free!"

although they wrote it down

it has never come to be

we have always

known the truth behind the lie

13. 13

It was a moment called freedom
wordplay, before the ink was dry

new plans to keep slaves marching in place
into unmarked graves

Mississippi burning, Oklahoma to southern states
lost the war, now they have a new flame

KKK that's the name
writing books . . . how to keep the negro a slave
have you read it?
segregation planted the seeds of discord across the nation

"just give them a little more; maybe integration?
call it civil rights . . . we can kill them differently
no one will know, you see
they write the history

14. 1492

Old world discovers new
land we already walked

Africa touching the world
Pangea seeds planted

pyramid dreams
all over

this sun never sets
on our journey to our glory

1492
new world order

2016 is a false reality
portrayed real

maybe one day someone
will tell the truth

15. Speak the Truth

Today, like yesterday
the world has changed

tomorrow's future eyes open
see whatever you want
make a better way

do not dwell on a past reborn
or watch the world go by
this is your chance
to get it right

speak your truth, then live it
because dead men
don't lie

16. A New Name

We have survived your best
at our worst
still you want more
as if our soul was not enough

the things you seem to value:
segregation
voting rights
ghetto life
not just me but poor whites

you want to be me
yet try to extinguish the light
drug warfare, push welfare
on the disenfranchised

then you change the laws to suit you
call it what you want
give it a new name
it's still racism

17. The Take Out

The Democrats didn't win
(damn, free college!)

gone until we get them back in

the GOP wasted 87 mill
trying to repeal your medical bill

up, up, and away

January 21st, every day since
they tout that border control wall

(I mean Border Patrol fence)

18. Private Institutions

Nothing new

the same story under review
this is how America got you
prison pipeline, Black Gold
Incarcerated, black souls

Institutions, and schools
commit crimes against you
the all new Jim Crow
back to plantation rule you

his mission: 1972
build them
fill them
replace them

repeat

19. Painting America

Making America great again is America's greatest sin
return to a past, come back to life, driven by corrupt men

no future status, just stinking Lazarus

our leaders sing words that don't mean a thing
and the people wish on history's dreams: "oh say can you see?"

I can

don't underestimate my silence. overstand you have brought me to violence

seeing you have never paid restoration for your past crimes, your bill is come due

don't be surprised when we commence to painting America insurrection blue

The Man

20. Riding High

I am a story waiting to be told
with every word you say
free my soul

find the vision, know it well
be inspired by truth
everyday

I am Malcolm, I am King
I am Ancestor, I am We
We are you

claim it, speak it, live it
say it loud: I'm Black
and I'm proud

21. The Echoes

Can you hear it? listen...

calling out are the whispers of a thousand years
the cry of ancestors, long forgotten
speak truth untold, unwritten

seldom mentioned

I am Mankind
in divine dimensions
my earth tone bleeds in rainbow Melanin

no longer will I live this lie
no longer will I forsake the cries
my brethren, our Abel from the dust

can you hear the echo of dark man blues?

22. The Game

if it were me
I would not be diminished by the game
or a checker to forget I'm a King

watch yourself
get big
get checked

remind the others they could be next
if u don't walk the line
that's game time.

unless,
they have conditioned
your mind: check mate

23. The Symbol

I have pledged my allegiance
spoke its name
although it has no soul

we are taught to surrender to it
this symbol of a freedom
we have not seen

it speaks of liberty, I seek its justice

I may never live it
I have even fought for it

its truth has no voice
words from the past
do not represent me

this knowledge is a vessel
food for the mind
digest it

don't waste it

24. The Illusion

Wrong place, wrong time
America's bad rhyme
is history playing itself out again

another soul taken
"I feared for my life" that same old song
after they shoot another one
Dead

now here's the illusion:
"he looks like a bad dude"

without a gun

you've been categorized
too much threat, too dark
but the sun cannot be undone

25. Man's Last Chance

The earth speaks
she calls out in storm

we are so out of harmony
we great lake in small pond
when nature meant us to river

mankind so emotional a creature
warring over man-made religion, race, creed
damn the color of our skin! are we not one seed?

this may be man's last chance to turn the page
a final age; can someone tell me

who's going to save
the seed?

26. No Reply

Face the Nation
        Status:

redefine who I am
my legal standing
still second class
I thought I had rights

I've come to this understanding
America never kept its word
no justice, not even a trail
shot dead for the color of my skin

with or without you
this has to end
the only virus upon this land
must be purged

27. A Different Me

I come anew
unlike any other
I am distinct and diverse
one day someone will write about me
tell the world he made love beautiful again

with an open mind
love one another
without judgment

give thought as to why
I share my heart
always remember, it could be you
on the outside looking in
asking the question:

why me?

28. Self, Conversation

It was a moment
to have this talk with myself
I needed to think out loud
before speaking truth; not everyone will agree

you see we all think differently
this world we live in
on the verge of coming
to an end as we know it

the way we see each other
with our eyes open and yet, our minds
are still closed
yes, I needed this moment to think out loud

to wonder: does anyone else think like me?
the way we're playing it
someone else will write our history
and Black will be no more

29. Tellin' You Something

Can you hear the echo?
America's undercover story
true colors fly in 2016

this is not a dream
wake up my people. they
out to get you without a chance

"Take them out, as many as you can!"
Trump got them riled up
speaking what they truly feel
we have had enough of this pill
they stay making plans to kill
to the theme song
"Make America Great Again"

Listen to the code words:

Somebody Tellin' You Something
pay attention

30. Color Lines

I see you
pity you don't see me
even though I bear your
forefather's name

caught up in a cycle
wish it were a dream
nightmares never come to good end
in a dead man's game

seek the same rights
trying with
all my might
to treat you the same

the rules you made up
didn't included my make up
in that thing you call
the American dream

31. Happenstance

It is something I see everyday
painting images in my mind
this could be me

it's not hard to picture
on the streets of L.A
all eyes on me and yet no one hears

"Do you have any change?"
passed by like a billboard sign
too fast to read

it still goes through my mind
I still hear the words
"spare a dime"

this is Americas sin
this life we are living
just a paycheck away

32. Audience Participation

Bigotry now the spoken norm,
I guess it was time to pay it forward
unaffected by truth
emboldened by trump and the hate he spoke
he mouthpiece in stereo so
they would not have to

but, see the big picture:
where was my input?
where was my voice?

audience participation manipulated
in this election
don't cry now, you've made your choice
forty-three percent made it clear and
smiling, ran headlong toward this end

go ahead.
step in frontline formation
protest the monster of your own making
this is now your life

33. Stagnant

It would seem Mankind has no purpose
nor has he tried to improve
his state of being
to look beyond the surface

Suppressed trust undermines enlightenment
refusal to use his gift
to bring forth better existence

it would seem this life is on u-turn
colliding with destiny
Man's unwillingness to show courage
in this millennium

it was written
the meek shall inherited the earth
a fallacy, a myth
to give hope where there is none

it would seem
the greatest gift man has to offer
may never be received

34. Dark Man Blues

See the world as I

mind open, played out
in full view of society

picture me through time
from ruling, to   slavery

locked in an actuality
that is not my own

I define my history
true perspective laid out   a c r o s s c e n t u r i e s

Live the skin I'm in
Know I am a King!

live my destiny, my life
I'd like to see you try and
                      live these...

Dark Man Blues

The Blues

35. Echoes of You

I am driven to live
every word, each hunger

I am an emotional creature
passion make me, love, take me

grow like thunder
in the center of your storm

the moment you cease to whirlwind
I will become the voice of peace
echoing

36. Your Mind

I thought about this line
I would speak it
like I want to make love
to your mind
like love song made up of only
your name
come here. whisper your fantasy as if
we were the poem

37. Loving You

I'm going to love you
with all my senses,
not just the five they mention

we, in 360 dimensions
encompass this love

you and I are the world
my complicated passions
leave traces
of this existence

in this oneness
we share surrender
awake as echoes
dreams for all to see

this is our masterpiece
the greatest work of art

38. The Lines

Read me, find me
playing with words

World Stage press your
thumbs into each page

feed your imagination
open doors to expression

taste of this melanin driven
temptation, making dreams

along these lines
one. word. at. a. time.

39. Open Pages

Knowing you the way I do
I am scripting my affection

a blueprint to love you
just the way you want
you are the real thing

gazing into your dreams
I have read the pages
of your heart

they whisper your surrender
I dare you to imagine
the possibilities

40. Never Can Say No

Love called
said she missed me (I miss you too)

she woke me from a dream
my want echoed

she is daily
like the sun chasing the moon

singing
(I could never say no)

love called
said she needed some attention

said my time would be
her only mission

said she wanted to tempt me
brought my heart to the verge of asking:

"have you always felt this way?"
love answered

41. Anticipation

She needed a distraction
she needed complicated passions

I began to caress her imagination,
one thought at a time

the words seem to take her
beyond anticipation

"how do you love me,
after you make love 2 me?"

my emotions danced in her mind
I could sense something beautiful

inside of her moments
we found my dreams

suddenly, we were living
our best reality

42. My Lovely You

surrender the sun to the moon
contemplating how beautiful

you flower announcing spring
you summer shower I waited for

you autumn gold and orange glow
you foreshadow the wintery fire

    you unconventional ease
    my lovely you

43. The Rest of My Life

I love your hair
        and the way you wear it

I would love to take it down
        run my fingers through it

to look into your eyes
        I would gaze with delight

your lips I would kiss until I got it right
        I want to be in every word you speak

I want to be your living fantasy
        as I explore every hill, valley, and peak too

I won't stop until I discover every part of you
        that inside view

it's your imagination
        I'm in to

44. Did You Know?

I need to show you something, in
the unspoken words between these lines

anticipation without hesitation
no indecision in my thoughts

our love is primal. Sensing
the hunger, love's danger

"yes" is everything
my name echoes in your dreams

waking just to take you once again
did you know you are the love poem

I never want to end?

45. Finding Complicated Passions

I've been called many names and
they all please me
sharing what love should be

helping to find
the lover in you
search every moment

passion is
for making dreams
and maybe babies

if it's a sin
we can stay friends
and still get it in

here's to us
finding your
complicated passions

46. Off Paper Love

I slept with poetry last tonight
caressed her surrender
like a dream
came true
had my emotions taken
by pleasure
I hear her affectionate whisper
complicated passions
you're a freak
she would take me deep
no intention of ever letting go
her wordplay
was my submission
no options' given
I only needed my pen
to go all in
one word next line
scripting this dope rhyme
I slept with poetry last night
because she made love
to my mind

47. Where I'm Coming From

I have the emotions of a love poem
charming wordplay to tease the mind

at times I find we are adrift on a
complicated river

truth is, this passion
makes me complete

feel the essence of my soul
drowning deep in you

that's where
I'm coming from

48. Exposed

You are become
the rhythm of my life

the music of my heart
played on the tip of my tongue

I am the kiss that
echoes throughout

you expose me
my every deep

49. Captured

I imagine romancing the day away
lost in thoughts of how
beautiful you are
I imagine seeing you
my every morning smile

I imagine embracing your spring tenderness
taking your next breath as my own
-so sensuous a drowning-
your body flows
with every echo of my name

I imagine whispering our love
passionately
the night will once again
consume us
I could never let go

50. The Biggest Part of Me

I have never loved this deep

until I had you in my arms
tempted by your charm

knowing I could not resist
becoming every moment
I dreamed

loving you into ecstasy
into words I could never say
your emotions tell me
how much you want me too

51. Writing to Her

Like a love song
the mystery in her eyes
stays tuned to FM

her frequency
verbalizing affections
making them my own

like the hook in a love song
she is the R&B poem
I want to take home

you turn me on
so let's write this poem
like a love song

52. Love and The Condition

She wanted my attention
living embodiment of every moment I spoke about

thought she could turn me out with passion
as though I was not

so, I became a small surrender
my thoughts, a sin

she whispered: "you need to give in"
we were the moments I dream

intimate kisses at arm's length
she's going to miss me

but next time, she'll want this
without conditions

53. Loving You: part 2

I going to love you with all my senses
not just the five they mention

in 360-degree dimensions
to inhale your essence

just to feel how the air moves
around you

to capture the melodies of your heartbeat
reaching out to the vibrations surrounding me

the moment I begin to discover your harmony
like a blind man would do

you turn the page...

54. A Blind Man's Story

I'm going to taste your intentions
from kiss to confession

to arouse your femininity
encompass your emotions

embrace your thoughts
paint the aura of your dreams

you exist at the breath edge
of my every thought

if only you could see yourself
the way I do

55. Mad Love

You mad, Love?

heart racing, pulse pounding
that sound in between each beat
is where I want to take your mind

one
thought
at a time

here.
give me that same old feeling
let me make it all better

56. Only Room 4 2

we took in the picture from a distance
somehow, you had my attention
my mind filled with words
I can't even mention

and all because of this view
(only room 4 2 in Room 42)

I know we're friends now
but I was thinking:
we could just
give in

and make take two
our sequel
again

57. Open Dialogue

Love called

wanted a conversation
said she had intentions of
being the dream I come home to

she began to undress my imagination
I could feel her under my skin
breaking down my resistance

picturing the moment I would give in
love said: "when you're ready to talk
just say my name"

58. Safari

I baited danger with charm

she captivated me
and I,
I was consumed by my own hunger

the hunt was on

she whispered: *"I know you want me."*
silence...
I became my next breath

found myself overtaken

she read my eyes, they spoke aloud
and I,
I knew I had become her prey

59. Word Remedy

We all flow differently
some flow rhymes and call it therapy
I make love to your mind
I just need a little of
your time

60. Beautiful Blindness

She outplayed me
like a words'
temptation

the look
her eyes
that smile

blind anticipation
I was ready for this,
and – in that

adjusted view –
contemplated
the next

moment

61. Like Music

You sing into me and I come alive

the fire in your body engulfs

the deeper of my soul

and I hear you,

like music

62. Playing Temptation

She was that first drink
she became my last

drunk with her moreness
consumed on empty stomach

intoxicated and swaying
from pleasures of a kiss

like the hook in a love song
"play me again"

like a fantasy
chasing the night away

she's got me
gone

63. Complicated Passions After Midnight

My overflow thoughts
imagination wander
into the deep of you

uncomplicate this passion
and I will hold time until
the last line surrenders

after midnight
I am the morning,
come

64. Lost Inside of You

I know your heartbeat
from the echo

I drown in your whispers
when you say my name

come find me

65. The Written Confessions Of DMB

These spoken truths
share something beautiful
chase the written wonder
into your lovely destination
I channel your affections

become what you dream

every pleasure is pout and
smoldering; you were
my canvas, and the
caressing thought

being taken by
the scent
of you

just to confess my love

66. Love Wants an Answer

Love came knocking

asking could she be the answer
to the moments beyond my complications?

written all over me
were the traces only she could see

if she wanted my thoughts
she would have to surrender her dreams

to reality

67. The Tale of Dark Man Blues

I am the night you long for
6 days of wandering
think me a dream
calling out

in a world of misunderstanding
we are what love should be

say you love me
bring temptation

the stories you write about
dare to become the moments
I become writing on the pages
of a never-ending line

the tales of
Dark Man Blues

68. The Bridge

Nobody wanted me until
someone had me

my role, my soul
my intentions, my love
without condition

true to myself
I love this one like
no one else

I cannot fall prey to the game when
I already have someone
whispering my name

giving positive time
building that relation bridge

69. The Whisper of My Name

Poetry is my soul

the word flow takes me

like the ever-changing weather

I take chances on this romance

I make love to your mind

one page at a time

just enough for you to give in

loving you like

insatiable

mischievous

I know how much I need you

70. Something About Me

She said she loved me and yet
she married the other guy
she asked me would we
still be friends
I told her
this was our end
I wouldn't cross this line

I had to erase her from my dreams
having them would complicate me

why
would never be my question
she was never my answer

loving her as I loved myself
seems to have been
my only weakness
living life emotional
it seems, my status quo

71. My Next Book

She would read me
capture my emotions as if they were her own

lines seem to come together, exposing hunger
like low rumbles in the pit of my stomach

she read me, and
I became an open book

the conversation lifted
I could feel my imagination swell

we would come together
lock-join like pieces within the same puzzle

I made her body
the title of my next book

from the book
"Imagining Freedom"

Evolve

She has long tried to paint herself
as the greatest place in the world

I've seen the pictures, America in
selfie-changing shades, masquerades as freedom

expose hidden thoughts
reluctant to confront her true self

"that's not me!"
she denies what history has shown us and yet

we believe she cannot, will not repeat her past
but we are the animals killing the animals

one day we will kill ourselves
while waiting for the next generation to evolve

from extinction

bonus poem:

being the moments
I dream
sharing me

this reflection my love's reality
a mirror of emotions
echoing every dare I can

living me
call it passion
become it if you want to

I'll never let go
seeing you're the reflection
of who's loving me

A Reflection of Who I Am

Dark Man Blues gray edition
Written by:
Samuel Rain Benjamin and Eric DeVaughnn

formatted and edited by:
Eric DeVaughnn

cover concept:
Samuel Rain Benjamin

cover design:
Eric DeVaughnn

Coming Soon:

Dark Man Blues: John Bold
The Love of Dark Man Blues

Dark Girl Magic

She dark girl
   magic

it wasn't her
appearance
I fell into,

what makes
me want to

   taste her inner
      beauty.

      She *moves* me

         sweetness, deep
            like blues

            if she only knew
               my surrender

               she dark-girl-
               stay-lovin' me

www.ingramcontent.com/pod-product-compliance
Lightning Source LLC
Chambersburg PA
CBHW042309150426
43198CB00001B/22